Elephants in DANGER

by Helen Orme

Consultant: The Born Free Foundation

BEARPORT
PUBLISHING

New York, New York

Credits
t=top, b=bottom, c=center, l=left, r=right
Corbis: 20–21, 22–23, 30. Shutterstock: OFC, 1, 2, 4–5, 6–7, 8–9, 10–11, 12, 14, 18–19, 25t, 25b, 26–27, 28–29, 32. Superstock: 10b, 12–13, 15, 16–17.
Every effort has been made to trace the copyright holders, and we apologize in advance for any unintentional omissions. We would be pleased to insert the appropriate acknowledgments in any subsequent edition of this publication.

Library of Congress Cataloging-in-Publication Data

Orme, Helen.
  Elephants in danger / by Helen Orme.
      p. cm. — (Wildlife survival)
  Includes bibliographical references and index.
  ISBN-13: 978-1-59716-260-9 (library binding)
  ISBN-10: 1-59716-260-4 (library binding)
  ISBN-13: 978-1-59716-288-3 (pbk.)
  ISBN-10: 1-59716-288-4 (pbk.)
  1. Elephants—Juvenile literature. I. Title. II. Series.

  QL737.P98O76 2007
  599.67—dc22

                                2006012272

For more information, write to Bearport Publishing Company, Inc., 101 Fifth Avenue, Suite 6R, New York, New York 10003. Printed in the United States of America.

10 9 8 7 6 5 4 3 2 1

The Wildlife Survival series was originally developed by ticktock Media Ltd.

Table of Contents

The Biggest

Elephants are the largest **mammals** that live on land. These clever animals can survive in many different **habitats**. They can live in the open **savannahs** of Africa or in the forests of Asia.

Elephants can even survive in deserts. Some elephants that live in the deserts of Namibia, Africa, may drink water only once every three to four days. These elephants are also experts at searching for food, which is hard to find in deserts.

There are two types of elephants, the African and the Asian.

A family of African elephants

African Elephants

Of the two kinds of elephants, African elephants are larger. They live in the southern part of Africa, on open plains and dry deserts. Some African elephants live in forests.

In parts of Africa, there are still plenty of elephants. However, even these animals are under threat from **poaching**, farming, and **climate** changes.

Two young male elephants practice fighting with their small tusks.

Both male and female African elephants have tusks. They use them for digging up roots to eat. Males also use their tusks for fighting.

Asian Elephants

Asian elephants live in many countries in Southeast Asia. They live mostly in forests, but they're also found on **grasslands** and in mountain areas.

Asian elephants have much smaller tusks and ears than African elephants. Female Asian elephants do not have tusks at all.

Asian elephants have been used as working animals for hundreds of years. They are much easier to train than African elephants.

Elephant Life

Females, called cows, and young elephants live in family herds. The herds often join with one another to make **clans**.

Females start to have **calves** when they are between 10 and 13 years old. All the cows in the herd help look after the babies.

Male elephants are called bulls. They leave the herd when they're about 13 years old. They either live alone or in a **bachelor group** with other males.

Female elephants are pregnant for 22 months. No other mammal has a longer pregnancy.

Finding Food

Elephants feed on different types of plants, including grass, leaves, branches, fruit, farm crops, and tree bark. They eat huge amounts every day and need a big area to **forage** for food.

Elephants are very clever at finding water. They use their tusks to dig for it in the ground. Their digging makes water holes that many other animals can also use. Each elephant drinks around 50 gallons (189 l) of water every day.

Babies drink their mothers' milk. They use their mouths, not their trunks, to **suckle**.

Amazing Trunks

An elephant's trunk is an overgrown nose and lip. African elephants have two "fingers" at the end of their trunks. Asian elephants have one "finger." The "fingers" can tell whether an object is big or small and hot or cold. They can also tell the shape of something.

Trunks are very useful for putting food into the mouth or for sucking up water. To drink, a young elephant must learn how to pour the water from its trunk into its mouth.

Elephants often use their trunks like a shower to squirt water. Sometimes they also blow dirt onto their backs for a dust bath.

*An Asian
elephant's trunk*

Tusks

Elephant tusks are just very long teeth. If an elephant loses a tusk it will be difficult for it to dig for water or roots, an important food. Baby elephants get their first real tusks when they are about two years old. Before that, they grow tiny tusks that are about two inches (5 cm) long. These are called milk tusks.

 The largest elephant tusk found was 11.5 feet (3.5 m) long. It weighed 214 pounds (97 kg)—the weight of a large man!

Working Elephants

Elephants have been used as working animals for thousands of years. Asian elephants have carried people and pulled heavy loads. They have even taken soldiers into war. Today, many working elephants are no longer needed because their work is done by machines.

In some countries, looking after **retired** elephants is a big problem. The elephants have to live in **sanctuaries** or **wildlife reserves** because they don't know how to look after themselves in the wild.

Some elephants have even learned how to paint! Their paintings are sold to raise money to look after retired elephants.

A tame, working elephant giving
a ride to tourists in India

Killing Elephants for Ivory

African elephants are in danger because people have often killed them for food and for their **ivory** tusks. The tusks are very valuable because ivory is easy to carve into beautiful objects. Hundreds of thousands of elephants have been killed so that people can sell ivory to make money.

Today, elephants are protected. It is against the law to buy or sell new objects made from ivory.

Unfortunately, many poachers ignore the laws that protect elephants. The animals continue to be killed for their tusks.

These elephant tusks were taken away from poachers and burned so that they couldn't be sold.

21

A Safe Place to Live

Elephants are starting to lose their habitats. People are changing the elephants' land into farms. Places in the forest where elephants live and find food are being destroyed by **logging**.

Wildlife reserves give elephants a safe place to live. However, these animals need lots of food. If the reserves are too small, the elephants eat everything too quickly. Plants can't grow back fast enough.

In order to save the elephants, people need to work together. They need to make sure that laws are enforced. They also need to find land that these gigantic animals can live on safely.

Humans cut down trees on the elephants' land to sell the wood for money. The wood can be used as fuel or to make paper.

Where Do Elephants Live?

- African elephants live in forests, deserts, and on savannahs. These areas are marked in red on the map.

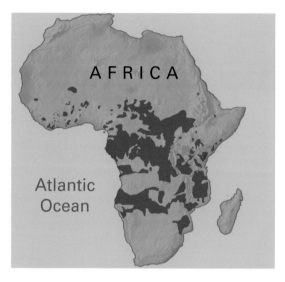

- Asian elephants live in forests, open grassy areas, and on mountains. These areas are marked in yellow on the map.

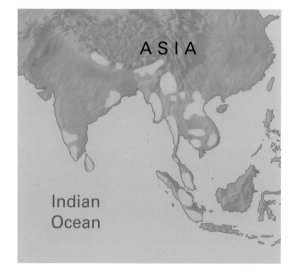

More About Elephant Bodies

- An elephant's trunk can grow up to 7 feet (2 m) long and weigh as much as 309 pounds (140 kg). A trunk has more than 100,000 muscles and no bones.

- Elephants can hold up to 2 gallons (6 l) of water in their trunks.

- If an elephant is in deep water, it can use its trunk to breathe—like a snorkel!

- Elephants live to be 65 to 70 years old.

- Elephants have wide, padded feet, which means they can walk very quietly.

African elephants
Weight: 8,818 to 15,432 pounds
(4,000 to 7,000 kg)
Height: 10 to 13 feet (3 to 4 m)

Asian elephants
Weight: 6,614 to 13,228 pounds
(3,000 to 6,000 kg)
Height: 7 to 11.5 feet (2 to 3.5 m)

More About Elephant Families

- The leader of each elephant family is called the matriarch. She is the largest, oldest, and wisest cow in the group.

- Elephants will look after weak or injured members of their clan.

- Female elephants give birth about once every 4 years.

- When calves are born, they are big. They weigh about 220 pounds (100 kg).

More About Elephant Food

- Elephants eat mostly plants, which don't supply a lot of energy. Elephants digest only about 40 percent of what they eat. They need a lot of food each day to keep from starving to death.

- Asian elephants eat bananas, bamboo, berries, mangoes, coconuts, corn, jungle shrubs, palm fruits, sugar cane, and wild rice. African elephants eat mainly leaves, grass, and roots.

- Elephants like salty things. They look for salty-tasting rocks and lick them to get the salt they need.

More About Elephants in Danger

- Some people think it's a good idea to cut off elephants' tusks so that poachers won't kill them. However, elephants need their tusks to get food. Also, part of each tusk is inside the animal's head. Poachers may still kill elephants to get to that part.

- Elephants once lived across Asia. However, because of too much hunting, fewer than 100,000 Asian elephants are left in the world.

How many African elephants are left?	
Year	Number Left
1979	1.3 million
1989	600,000
2002	400,000
2010	?

Conservation

- Wildlife reserves aren't always successful. Some don't have fences around them because they are too expensive to put up. Without fences, however, elephants can wander away and poachers can easily get in.

- Some people think that reserves have been too successful. The number of elephants has gone up in some places, but now there is not enough food for the animals. Without food, elephants often go onto farms and eat crops, which makes farmers very angry.

- Many local people don't like the reserves. They think they take up land that could be used to grow food.

- One way to get humans and elephants to live together is to get local people involved in wildlife tourism. **Tourists** need places to stay, guides, and food. When local people provide these things, they make money. It then becomes important to them to keep the elephants safe.

Tourists on vacation watch elephants roam.

How to Help

Conservation is everyone's job. There are many ways to help elephants:

- Learn more about elephants. Teach others at school about the importance of helping them.

- Help an organization, such as the African Wildlife Foundation (AWF) (www.awf.org). Groups such as this one raise money to pay for conservation work. To help the AWF or another conservation group, have a yard sale. Sell old clothes, toys, and books. Then donate the money that is made to the group.

- Ask your teacher if your class can adopt an elephant. (Don't worry, it won't live in your classroom.) Go to a reliable Web site, such as shop.awf.org/adopt/, to see how to adopt a baby elephant or a herd of elephants.

Visit these Web sites for more information on elephants and how to help them:

www.pbs.org/wnet/nature/elephants/
www.sheldrickwildlifetrust.org/
www.worldwildlife.org/elephants

Glossary

bachelor group (BACH-uh-lur GROOP) several young male elephants living together

calves (KAVZ) young elephants

clans (KLANZ) several large groups of elephant families

climate (KLYE-mit) having to do with the weather

conservation (*kon*-sur-VAY-shuhn) the protection of wildlife, forests, and natural resources

forage (FOR-ij) to look for food in the wild

grasslands (GRASS-landz) dry areas covered with grass where only a few bushes and trees grow

habitats (HAB-uh-*tats*) places in the wild where animals or plants live

ivory (EYE-vur-ee) the hard material that forms elephant tusks

logging (LOG-ing) the cutting down of trees for wood

mammals (MAM-uhlz) warm-blooded animals that have hair and nurse their offspring

poaching (POHCH-ing) hunting illegally on someone else's land in order to capture or kill an animal so that it can be sold for money

retired (ri-TYE-urd) no longer working

sanctuaries (SANGK-choo-*er*-eez) safe places for animals to live where they are protected from hunters

savannahs (suh-VAN-uhz) large, open areas of land in Africa where grasses and bushes grow

suckle (SUHK-ul) when an animal draws liquid into its mouth by using its tongue and lips

tourists (TOOR-ists) people who are on vacation

wildlife reserves (WILDE-life ri-ZURVZ) protected areas where the killing of animals or the cutting down of trees is against the law

Index